THE RETAIL STORE AS THEATER

continued

INTRODUCTION

When the first merchant in old Baghdad or Babylon started to rearrange his copper pots and pans so that they would sparkle in the sunlight and perhaps catch a passer-by's eye, — he was creating "Theater". The first retail theatrical setting might have been the rich, deeply colored Oriental rug that was placed on the ground under the displayed merchandise. The hustle and bustle — the razzle-dazzle and the coming and going of the ancient bazaars was "theater". Wherever and whenever there is presentation — or display — there is "theater".

In today's lexicons, "theater" is synonymous with excitement — entertainment — make-believe — new — fun — fireworks and flamboyance — far-out and trendy. Theater is "where it is happening" — "where 'they' go" — "where to be"; it is where to meet — to see and to be seen. Theater is where, if even for a short while, anyone in the audience can become the star and take bows to a standing ovation. Theater is "day dreaming" — and "dreams come true".

In our current "laid back" society in which so many suffer, in varying degrees, from lethargy and ennui and their popular anthem could be the "Shake me-Wake Me-Entertain Me Blues", — Theater is the panacea — the cure all for all their ills. It is the escape into a better world — it is the "somewhere over the rainbow". If, today, Dorothy — with Toto on the leash — were to start off to find Oz and her heart's desire, all she would have to do is follow the yellow line on the macadam paved road to the nearest shopping mall, strip or center. That is where "dreams come true" — that is where "it is at". That is where Theater is today — or it should be!

Unfortunately, not all retailing and retail operations are creating the excitement of Theater. Too many are just plain dull and boring; selling new merchandise in tired, old settings without highlights and shadows, — without sparkle and shimmer, — without Drama and Display! They do not beckon to the shopper. They do not entice or excite. They don't stimulate the shopper. Laid back or bored as the consumers are — consumers they still are and consume they must. Buy, wear and use they will, but only what and where they are turned on. The selling mood has to be created; — the proper ambience, — the right setting, — properly lit and merchandised in a visually stimulating style.

continued

"Stores Of The Year, Vol.III" presents — "The Retail Store as Theater". It hopes to supply the program notes on how merchants and store planners are coping — and adding theater to the shopping experience. In the 300 or more photographs that were selected from the thousands taken all over the United States, Canada, Mexico, Europe and Japan, we have endeavored to illuminate and illustrate the synopsis of our production; What's "in"? What's "out"? What is going up and what is coming down? What is being shown — and how is it being shown? What are the new interior colors? What textures and materials are being used in which areas? Are mannequins more important than ever? Who is using the realistic kind — who is using the abstract — and where and how? Are there other ways of displaying merchandise effectively? Are ceilings coming down and are mezzanines going up? What kind of lighting is being used — how is it being used and where? How has power conservation become a design asset? Have fixtures changed? Are there new concepts in the reuse of old or existing structures? How important is Rehabilitation and Retrofitting in tired, old operations? How much of an inroad has Post Modernism made on the Merchandising scene?

In what follows we hope you will find the answers to these "cliff-hanger" questions as well as ideas on how to adapt the following spectaculars into smaller, "off-Broadway", commercial successes. So, — take your seats, — the curtain is going up on "The Retail Store as Theater"; the newest SHOW in town that stars the merchandise and features the trend-setting settings.

Martin M. Pegler, ASID/ISP

INDEX of ADVERTISERS

ACKNOWLEDGMENTS

MARTIN M. PEGLER, Consultant, who selected the photos and wrote the copy.

HERBERT KEHL, Art Director, who designed the book.

FRAN PIRONE POCHTRAGER, Assistant Editor.

WENDY VOLIN COHEN, Production.

MARITZA RODRIGUEZ, Who set the type.

Majority of Photographs by: SANFORD LITWAK, Sandy L. Studios, New York City.

*We are grateful to the following photographers for their
contributions to STORES OF THE YEAR, Volume III*

Marvin Rand, Los Angeles, CA
Daniel Cornish, New York, NY
Gil Amiaga, New York, NY
Paul Warchol, Brooklyn, NY
Scott Frances, New York, NY
Nick Wheeler, Townsend Harbor, MA
O. Baitz, Cliffwood, NJ
Lynne Reynolds, New York, NY
Victoria Lefcourt, Baltimore, MD
Bielenberg, Los Angeles, CA

Dick Busher, Seattle, WA
Lucy Rahmer, Toronto, Ontario, Can.
Leslie Gill, New York, NY
Phill LaRocco, Denver, CO
Dan Forer, North Miami, FL
Daniel Cohen, Hoboken, NJ
John McNanie, New York, NY
Chengyen Lee, San Francisco, CA
John Wadsworth, Norfolk, VA
Toshi Yoshimi, Los Angeles, CA

Maguire Productions, Akron, OH
Tom Crane, Brynmawr, PA
Derrick & Love, New York, NY
Norman McGrath, New York, NY
Jim Norris, Chicago, IL
Michael Roberts, Chicago, IL
Darwin Davidson, New York, NY
Michael Datoli, New York, NY
Sandra Williams & Assoc., San Diego, CA

STORE FRONTS & FACADES

TRUMP TOWER, *New York, NY*

Broad expanses of clear glass — rich marble — or familiar and friendly brick; cozy
little shop fronts that welcome you in or towering "palaces" that engulf you, — and it is all out
there and it is all Theater. Big "Broadway" block-busters or "off-Broadway" intimate
revues, — they are all out there tempting — beckoning — calling —
inviting you in. So, — let them entertain you!

HECHT'S, *Towson, MD*

ANN TAYLOR, *Boston, MA*

HUTZLER'S, *Baltimore, MD*

Bold, dynamic architectural facades that come on strong from across miles of parking lot with the names emblazoned in clear, easily read letters. These "sets" are designed to be just as effective in daylight or under night time flood lights.

BLOOMINGDALE'S, *King of Prussia, PA*

DAVISON'S, *Atlanta, GA*

PIED PIPER, *Manhasset, NY*

The smaller shop in the big mall needs to make a smart, eye-riveting effect. A clean, graphic design can do it. It can also be done with bright, colorful displays brought right up to the glass line, — well lit and well tended. The unexpected and the unusual treatment of big scale in small spaces strikes a great opening chord.

THE MUSEUM STORE, *Chicago, IL*

ANN TAYLOR, *Willow Grove, PA*

JULIUS LEWIS, *Memphis, TN*

ZOO SHOP, *Chicago, IL*

HEALTHWORKS, *New York, NY*

PALACIO DE HIERRO, *Mexico City, Mexico*

Some stores keep the curtain down during the overture,
there are no display windows and so they make their impact
and state their Image with the grand, physical effect of the
architecture. Other retailers let the shopper see the
"setting" and the "cast of characters" right from the very
start. They are appealing to a sense of intimacy as they
create their image and hoping to draw the
shopper into the plot of their drama.

Ideally, as the final notes of the overture are sounded and the curtain starts to rise — there should be a continuity — a refrain that flows through the store's opening into the interior and the selling space. See p.36.

UPPER MAD, *New York, NY*

DAYTON'S, *St Paul, MN*

OPENING DISPLAYS

DAIMARU, *Osaka, Japan*

Curtain up! It's SHOW-TIME and it's time to show what's new, — what's exciting — and what will make this week's performance different from last week's. Display is back, — by popular demand, — and the shoppers and store keepers alike are looking for it! With the street-facing windows becoming a rarity (though they are beginning to reappear in the rehabilitated urban stores), enclosed show windows are now appearing inside the store, — inside the mall. Often they are complete entities with dramatic lighting equipment and space for the props and accessories which might otherwise not be feasible on the open selling floor.

BLOOMINGDALE'S, *King of Prussia, PA*

MACY'S, *Stamford, CT*

DAVISON'S, *Atlanta, GA*

DAIMARU, *Osaka, Japan*

Displays climb to greater heights to gain attention; up on platforms — raised onto mezzanines or hoisted skyward on mirrored plinths. Props and plants add to the pizzaz while spotlights light up the action.

The enclosed glass display area protects the merchandise and the accessories from sticky fingers and thoughtless hands but still maintains the appeal of the classic show window.

ABRAHAM & STRAUS, *Willow Grove, PA*

JOHN HOGAN, *Newport, CA*

ABRAHAM & STRAUS, *King of Prussia, PA*

The shadowbox with a full background is a miniature version of the street show window — without the glare — and with completely controlled lighting within and without. The vignette setting on a platform — facing the oncoming traffic on the aisle — can become an effective "entrance" to a shop without the construction of walls, doors or arches.

PALACIO DE HIERRO, *Mexico City, Mexico*

FILENE'S, *Boston, MA*

JULIUS LEWIS, *Memphis, TN*

WOMEN'S WEAR
Ready-to-Wear, Separates, Dresses, Coats & Suits

Enters the star! A grand entrance into a multi-level and multi-faceted setting. The stage is set for the casual — the comfortable — for business wear — for warm weather or cool — for night or day. A large cast of characters is on hand. They keeps changing seasonally — and sometimes even more often. Sometimes the cast is interchangeable; you can't tell who is playing what without a program — or without good visual merchandising or display! Here are some highlights from the past few seasons; "Big Hits" where the Visual Merchandising and Display almost stole the show.

YVES SAINT LAURENT, *Manhasset, NY*

MAMMINA, *Tokyo, Japan*

Whether it is a "crowd scene" — or a duet centerstage, how the merchandise is presented and what it is presented on says much about the shop and the garments. Some merchandise calls out for a chorus of dozens alike, all lined up like the Rockettes, while others are more special and individual and need the emptier stage on which to play their scene.

ANN TAYLOR, *Bal Harbour, FL*

LINEA PITTI, *Washington D.C.*

The stage must be lit if the action is to be seen.
Incandescent spotlights play up the merchandise as well as the displays that
enhance the selling space.

BULLOCK'S, *Manhattan Beach, CA*

BYCK'S, *Louisville, KY*

If the ceiling is high then the accent lighting has to come down closer to the play area. Even if the lighting fixtures are visible — they don't necessarily slow down the action or intrude into the scene; they can become part of the decor.

LONNY'S, *Woodbury, NY*

NORDSTOM, *San Diego, CA*

FOLEY'S, *Memorial City, TX*

THE MAY CO., *Palm Desert, CA*

FOLEY'S, *Memorial City, TX*

"Face-outs" are the "stars" while the supporting cast does a professional and space saving "shoulder-out" routine below. Binning is sharp and orderly and an effective color-presentation technique. Well dressed and coordinated fixtures bring on the stock players. The set is bathed in flattering, warm light.

STREETS & CO., *New York, NY*

HECHT'S, *Towson, MD*

SEALFONS, *Ridgewood, NJ*

SWEATER COUNTRY

DAIMARU, *Osaka, Japan*

Mannequins take over for signs and identify the area and the type of merchandise for sale. They add a "look" and an "image"

BONWIT TELLER, *Manhasset, NY*

BULLOCK'S, *1000 Oaks, CA*

while performing the character roles that the shoppers can identify with. They are the salespeople who model while they sell.

MACY'S, *Stamford, CT*

ACT I: Scene II: *"On The Town"*

DESIGNER SHOPS, GOWNS & FURS

GIVENCHY, *New York, NY*

The Super-Stars! The brightest stars make their entrances up some stairs,
— on thick, oriental rugs, — surrounded by antique period furniture
(or expensive replicas), — mirrors, plants and soft, subtle lighting. Their names
appear on the marquee over the entrance — sometimes in lights — letting
the shopper know — "this is a star act" — "this is the big time!"

HOLT RENFREW, *Edmonton, Canada*

NORDSTROM, *Bellevue, WA*

Turn down the lights and turn up the action. Make it soft, — make it warm, — make it romantic. This setting has to appear special.

UPPER MAD, *New York, NY*

MACY'S, New York, NY

DAVISON'S, *Atlanta, GA*

FURLA, *New York, NY*

MOI LE CHIC, *Woodbury, NY*

FILENE'S, *Newington, NH*

A few well selected props can set the scene whether it be classic, country casual, or "from this moment on".

BAMBERGER'S, *Livingston, NJ*

LOEWE, *Trump Tower, NY*

BARNEY'S, *New York, NY*

DAYTON'S, *St.Paul, MN*

BONWIT TELLER, *Manhasset, NY*

GIVENCHY, *New York, NY*

Merchandise is presented with a light touch; — no heavy orchestrations — not too much brass (unless its in the fixturing) and just a gentle cadenza played in a few, well selected notes.

MARVIN RICHARDS, *Woodbury, NY*

ZOOM, *New York, NY*

JUNIOR SHOPS & TREND-SETTING SHOPS

CHARIVARI, *New York, NY*

The fast-stepping, high-kicking, stores of tomorrow
making a splashy entrance today. The newest of
the new; the freshest, sassiest and most daring
acts presented with verve, vivid color and a
vivacious cast of characters.

TOP SHOP, *Cambridge, England*

Far-out fixtures and fun displays go with the sharp lighting techniques and the pulsating music that fills these shops. They are young, bold and brassy.

THE GAP, *Paramus, NJ*

Soaring space is incorporated into the bright, high flying spirit of the merchandise and the merchandise presentation takes off with trapezes and superstructures. The mannequins reflect the same sprightly attitudes.

DAYTON'S, *St.Paul, MN*

BULLOCK'S, *Manhattan Beach, CA*

DIANNE B., *New York, NY*

New fresh colors and unorthodox displayers emphasize the "now" quality of the act. Merchandise is coordinated and accessorized so that the story line is easy to follow — and the fashions are easy to shop.

HIGH GEAR, *New York, NY*

STRAWBRIDGE & CLOTHIER, Ardmore, PA

BARNEY'S, *New York, NY*

49

CARNAVAL, *New York, NY*

There is a tempo to the Trend-Setting Shop; a beat and a bounce. Merchandise takes off into space, patterns play, there are graphics galore — and more and more merchandise coming at the shopper from unexpected spaces.

FOLEY'S, *Memorial City, TX*

LULU'S, *New York, NY*

DANCE CENTRE, *New York, NY*

The setting doesn't have to be cluttered and the music doesn't have to be loud, but they often go together in Junior Shops. Cutout forms and abstract mannequins wear the newest styles with a jaunty panache that can't be matched.

DAIMARU, *Osaka, Japan*

MARSHALL FIELD, *Dallas, TX*

LONNY'S, *Woodbury, NY*

COSMETICS & PERFUMES

ULTRA FEMME, *Cancuun, Mexico*

A love song lingers in the air. Spring is captured in a crystal
container and lovliness is everywhere. Flushed, flattering colors
flood the walls and floor of this magical setting where
everyone is beautiful — or can
be made beautiful.

SIBLEY'S, *Rochester, NY*

HECHT'S, *Towson, MD*

JOSEPH MAGNIN, *Torrance, CA*

THE DENVER, *Denver, CO*

Soft lamp lighting reflects off peach and pinkish floors
and fixtures to add to the glow of the setting. Shoji
screen brings in a strain from "Mme. Butterfly" —
as well as a touch of the exotic.

BLOOMINGDALE'S, *King of Prussia*

CRABTREE & EVELYN, *Washington D.C.*

Two extremes for two different audiences; a classic
English apothecary shop for classic soaps and scents,
contrasted with the trendy, spirited theatrics of the
new, colored cosmetics.

MACY'S, *New York, NY*

ABRAHAM & STRAUS, *King of Prussia, PA*

Plants, flowers and shaded lamps are as important
to the set dressing as the samplers, testers, mirrors and
point of purchase fixtures.

ERELLA, *West Bloomfield, MI*

JEWELRY

BLOOMINGDALE'S, *King of Prussia, PA*

The general lighting is turned down low and the
stars shine. Carefully directed spots and counter lights
add new brilliance and sparkle to the lines
the Jewelry has to speak. In this subdued setting, the
baubles, bangles and beads make a flashing
and glittering appearance.

STRAWBRIDGE & CLOTHIER, *Burlington, NJ*

SIBLEY'S, *Rochester NY*

FREDERIC GOODMAN, *Upper Mountclair, NJ*

SAKS FIFTH AVENUE, *Dallas, TX*

New Jewelry and body ornaments need new backgrounds to appear in. Even though the "theater" is old (a rehab) the scene is fresh and clean; white accented with blooming greens.

JEWEL MART, *Akron, OH*

DAVID CRAIG, *Langhorne, PA*

STRAWBRIDGE & CLOTHIER, *Ardmore, PA*

CHRISTIAN BERNARD, *King of Prussia, PA*

The light is directed where it is needed — and in well lit, shadowboxes there are exquisite arrangements of the precious beauties. The "girls in the back row" get a "front-row" treatment as they are individually highlighted for the audience's pleasure.

BULLOCK'S, *Manhattan Beach, CA*

ABRAHAM & STRAUS, *Willow Grove, PA*

The museum case is an ideal fixture and an ideal setting for a mini-extravaganza. It is where the small and precious make out — with close audience participation.

NORDSTROM, *Bellevue, WA*

HEADGEAR

A top performer that sometimes gets
lost in the fashion setting. To get
it into the spotlight requires display
and clever visual merchandising;
more than a hat-rack or a hat-tree.
Show hats and head-gear as fashion
accessories and color highlights
to top a costume.

STRAWBRIDGE & CLOTHIER, *Burlington, NJ*

ABRAHAM & STRAUS, *Willow Grove, PA*

HOSIERY

B.ALTMAN & CO., *Willow Grove, PA*

More than silk stockings, tights, anklets, or hose, — it's the whole range of leg coverings in myriad colors, patterns, textures and fibers. It's a chorus line of high-stepping legs. It's a series of skirt-raising skits and a full array of color keyed merchandise.

ABRAHAM & STRAUS, *King of Prussia, PA*

STRAWBRIDGE & CLOTHIER, *Burlington, NJ*

BAMBERGER'S, *King of Prussia, PA*

BAGS & BELTS

The supporting cast! The quick-change artists that can make a costume change by the addition of a new touch of color — or a dash of the trendy. The soft, supple seductresses that have to be seen to be appreciated.

FOLEY'S, *Memorial City, TX*

GARFINCKEL'S, *Washington D.C.*

The precious look, — behind glass. Displayed in fully lit counters or in museum cases; close enough to see but not to touch.

CLAIRE PEARONE, *Troy, MI*

Belts are displayed horizontally, as they are worn, but stocked and merchandised vertically for the economy of space and ease of the customer selection. Small leather goods usually snuggles up to the belts — and the bags are not far behind.

MACY'S, *Stamford, CT*

BYCK'S, *Louisville, KY*

LE SPORTSAC, *New York, NY*

BANBURY CROSS, *New York, NY*

The merchandise is dramatized and the accessory is accessorized with other "pretties" that enhance and underscore the importance of that accessory.

KNIT WIT, *Willow Grove, PA*

LOEWE, *Trump Tower, NY*

SHOES

VITTORIO RICCI, *New York, NY*

It's "Walking Happy" — and sitting comfortably in a warm, intimate setting. The merchandise steps into the spotlight, at eye level, and the audience settles back into the relaxed, muted ambience.

SAKS FIFTH AVENUE, *Dallas, TX*

BLOOMINGDALE'S, *King of Prussia, PA*

Ultra-modern or classic-chic, — from a rainbow fallout to an understated monochromatic story, the textures are rich and lovely to complement the fine leathers and fabrics.

CANDIE'S BAR,
White Plains, NY

DAYTON'S, *St. Paul, MN*

GARFINCKEL'S, *Washington D.C.*

ROSSETTI, *New York, NY*

77

KNIT WIT, *Willow Grove, PA*

HUTZLER'S, *Baltimore, MD*

PALACIO DE HIERRO, *Mexico City, Mexico*

BYCK'S, *Louisville, KY*

Risers are ever popular as they make stars out of the big cast of shoe styles. The mutilevel presentation sets the pairs of styles apart for the shopper to peruse with ease.

NORDSTROM, *San Diego, CA*

DAYTON'S, *St. Paul, MN*

FIELD BROTHERS, *Willowbrook, NJ*

Men's shoes are presented with style and the precision of a close order drill. The slick and savvy line-up is a real heel-clicker.

80

TO BOOT, *New York, NY*

BLOOMINGDALE'S, *King of Prussia, PA*

BARNEY'S, *New York, NY*

BATA INTERNATIONAL, *Vina del Mar, Chile*

LINGERIE & SLEEPWEAR

DESIGNER ONE LINGERIE, *Larchmont, NY*

Realistic or Romantic, — practical or just pretty, — it all happens in
this intimate, warm setting. Lights are turned down and the pinks and
peach-tones are turned up and it is definitely "A Woman's World".

HECHT'S, *Towson, MD*

WOODWARD & LOTHROP, *Baltimore, MD*

STRAWBRIDGE & CLOTHIER, *Burlington, NJ*

FOLEY'S, *Memorial City, TX*

SIBLEY'S, *Rochester, NY*

Mannequins shine in Lingerie. They give form and supply the figure for the soft, silky and lacy fashions. From pretty and realistic to striking and abstract, — they make more of the merchandise.

85

CENTERS OF INTEREST

Time to stretch! A time to absorb what has been seen and to separate that from what is yet to come. A pleasant walk in delightful surroundings. A change of scenery. The prologue to the next act — or the next level.

DAVISON'S, *Atlanta, GA*

ANN TAYLOR, *New York, NY*

DAYTON'S, *Atlanta, GA*

Whether it is up a level or down the aisle, it is a time to see and to be seen. It is a time for a relaxed, easy sell of merchandise in ever-changing display settings.

SAKS FIFTH AVENUE, *Dallas, TX*

THE BROADWAY, *Los Angeles, CA*

BAMBERGER'S, *King of Prussia, PA*

BARNEY'S, *New York*

A bit of center stage (or center of store) excitement and pizzaz with soaring, criss-crossing stairs or myriad lights and ceiling hung extravaganzas. It is the palette clearing "sherbet" in a banquet of "gourmet garments".

89

PALACIO DE HIERRO, *Mexico City, Mexico*

Up or Down, — sights to see — wonders to behold. An invitation to go on and discover more and more.

DAVISON'S, *Atlanta, GA*

YOUNKER'S, *Des Moines, IA*

MENSWEAR
Sportswear & Fashion Accessories

FIELD BROTHERS, *Huntington, NY*

"Make Room for Daddy" — and brother and son and hus-
band, and all those other fellows who have discovered
"Fashion", "brand names" and "Designer's labels". It's a
whole new show, with a whole new cast of sporty
characters.

MANSOURI, *Greenvale, NY*

ROBSON LTD. *Cherry Hill, NJ*

DAYTON'S, *St. Paul, MN*

The guys are getting the glamour treatment. The lines
may be classic or Traditional, but the interpretations
are chrome, mirror and sparkling new.

HOLT RENFREW, *Edmonton, Canada*

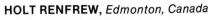

BARNEY'S, *New York, NY*

MICHAEL LEIGHTON, *Great Neck, NY*

Merchandise is getting a new slant with specially designed fixtures, and when the "name" is up in lights, — the store flaunts it. Colors are warmer and richer, — the textures are smoother and slicker. The settings are more sophisticated — less rustic.

STRAWBRIDGE & CLOTHIER, *Ardmore, PA*

Dramatic entrances are "in" as are mirrors and bold reflective surfaces.

FOLEY'S, *Memorial City, TX*

CLOTHES TO BOOT, *New York, NY*

BLOOMINGDALE'S, *King of Prussia, PA*

BAMBERGER'S, *King of Prussia, PA*

DAYTON'S, *St. Paul, MN*

DAYTON'S, *St. Paul, MN*

BULLOCK'S, *Manhattan Beach, CA*

Mannequins are taking over the Men's areas; some are realistic but more and more are semi-realistic (sculptured features without make-up). They appear in groupings, usually as threesomes, and often all in the same pose, — a kind of male "Chorus Line".

MANSOURI, *Greenvale, NY*

MACY'S, *Stamford, CT*

100

HIGH VOLTAGE, *Dallas, TX*

SIBLEY'S, *Rochester, NY*

THE DENVER, *Denver CO*

STRAWBRIDGE & CLOTHIER, *Burlington, NJ*

MACY'S, *Stamford, CT*

MARATHON, *New York, NY*

Big space or small space, the emphasis is on air and space; an open, uncluttered, easy-to-see and easy-to-shop space.

BAMBERGER'S, *Livinston, NJ*

ACTIVE SPORTSWEAR & UNISEX SHOPS

MARSHALL FIELD, *Chicago, IL*

Boys do it! Girls do it! — so "Let's Do It". Active Sportswear
is becoming big business as "leisure time" increases and
"leisure-wear" is "Designer-wear". Shops are appealing to
sports of both sexes, and the general look is white, bright
and fresh, sharp color.

ATHLEISURE, *King of Prussia, PA*

BAMBERGER'S, *King of Prussia, PA*

NIKE ONLY STORE, *Beaverton, OR*

DAYTON'S, *St. Paul, MN*

ABRAHAM & STRAUS, *Willow Grove, PA*

Semi-realistic mannequins in very active poses set the theme for these shops which are geared to the free and fun-loving spirits.

DAYTON'S, *St. Paul, MN*

DAIMARU, *Osaka, Japan*

BLOOMINGDALE'S, *King of Prussia, PA*

SPECTRUM SHOWCASE, *King of Prussia, PA*

THE BROADWAY, *Los Angeles, CA*

It's "lights — action — and more action". If two or three action mannequins don't tell the story, — the graphics will.

ZOO SHOP, *Lincoln Park Zoo, Chicago, IL*

FOLEY'S, *Memorial City, TX*

FOLEY'S, *Memorial City, TX*

BODY DESIGNS, *Stamford, CT*

BAMBERGER'S, *Livingston, NJ*

BONWIT TELLER, *Manhasset, NY*

BAMBERGER'S, *Livingston, NJ*

BODY DESIGNS, *Stamford, CT*

White is bright — and white makes an excellent foil for the bright, fresh color range of the merchandise. With or without mannequins, — the merchandise gets an attractive display, and the sharp diagonals do make an exciting directional statement.

DANCE CENTRE, *New York, NY*

CHILDREN'S WEAR

Up, up and away — and "Over The Rainbow" into a world of bright, primary colors and low scaled fixtures.

BLOOMINGDALE'S, *King of Prussia, PA*

BLOOMINGDALE'S, *King of Prussia, PA*

THE CHILDREN'S BOUTIQUE, *King of Prussia, PA*

STRAWBRIDGE & CLOTHIER, *Ardmore, PA*

T.V. screens to please their eyes, — oversized giraffes to capture their imagination, — and bleacher stands to win over the "little sports". It's all for them!

BULLOCK'S, *1000 Oaks, CA*

FOLEY'S, *Memorial City, TX*

STRAWBRIDGE & CLOTHIER, *Ardmore, PA*

BLOOMINGDALE'S, *King of Prussia, PA*

STRAWBRIDGE & CLOTHIER, *Ardmore, PA*

Lights and dazzle for young, sophisticated missies; sort of like big sister's — only different.

GIRLS 7-14

HECHT'S, *Towson, MD*

BONWIT TELLER, *Manhasset, NY*

MACY'S, *Stamford, CT*

ABRAHAM & STRAUS, *King of Prussia, PA*

BONWIT TELLER, *Manhasset, NY*

PEANUTS, *West Bloomfield, MI*

Just like Mommy; — boutiques and special shops for special merchandise — and Designer's names and brand names. Simple, modular components create a hi-tech interior with a ceiling that comes down to the little folks' level.

MACY'S, *Stamford, CT*

INTERMISSION: *"Wish You Were Here"*

AMBIENCE & AMENITIES

NORDSTROM, *San Diego, CA*

Another break. Another intermission. Some time
to sit out a friend's shopping spree — to take a spot of
tea, — slip off tight shoes from tired feet, —
or to relax and collect one's thoughts and
receipts.

VANITY FASHION, *Citrus Heights, CA*

YOUNKER'S, *Des Moines, IA*

THE BROADWAY, *Los Angeles, CA*

SEALFON'S, *Ridgewood, NJ*

CHINA, GLASS & GIFTWEAR

BULLOCK'S, *Manhattan Beach, CA*

The sparkle and shimmer of China & Glass, — the warmth
of crafted gifts and accessories for the home, — and the
unique shops for unique merchandise. An area low lit for
highlights, back lit for translucency and bottom lit for
brilliance.

STRAWBRIDGE & CLOTHIER, *Burlington, NJ*

FILENE'S, *Boston, MA*

127

Risers and tables are set for movable feasts for the eyes,
while glass etageres and mirror lined walls with glass
shelves reflect the best of the merchandise.

LONDON JEWELERS, *Greenvale, NY*

SIBLEY'S, *Rochester, NY*

MARSHALL FIELD, *Chicago, IL*

"Company" tonight! Make it special, — make it different, — but show the variety — the patterns — the sparkle and the cut. Changing eye-levels, good lighting, subdued settings and soft colorations combine to make this — "Entertainment"!

WOODWARD & LOTHROP, *Baltimore, MD*

ABRAHAM & STRAUS, *King of Prussia, PA*

MACY'S, *Stamford, CT*

DAVISON'S, *Atlanta, GA*

BULLOCK'S, *1000 Oaks, CA*

It is all in the lighting; from beneath, — from behind and from above. Risers, museum cases, glass shelves and accent colors make a crystal clear call to the shopper.

MARSHALL FIELD, *Chicago, IL*

BLOOMINGDALE'S, *King of Prussia, PA*

BLOOMINGDALE'S, *King of Prussia, PA*

GOURMET & KITCHEN

D.D.L. FOOD SHOW, *New York, NY*

Drama comes into the kitchen — and it's "cooking" with
spotlights, skylights and theatrical pizzaz. "Food" is the new
show in town, and everybody is getting into the act with new, eye-
catching, mouth-watering gimmicks, devices and displays.

DAIMARU, *Osaka, Japan*

STRAWBRIDGE & CLOTHIER, *Burlington, NJ*

BRANDEIS, *Omaha, NE*

BLOOMINGDALE'S, *King of Prussia, PA*

WOLFMAN GOLD & GOODS, *New York, NY*

MATSUYA, *Tokyo, Japan*

Supergraphics and super banners fill the soaring spaces. Hi-Tech
competes with country quaint and Milanese Modern for the
shopper's favor, — and anyway you slice it — the shopper is
the winner.

THE DENVER, *Denver, CO*

DEAN & DELUCA, *New York, NY*

Clutter vs. Crisp and Clean. It is the warmth of the old-fashioned delicatessen complete with pickle barrels and burlap bags — vs. the white and chrome uncluttered laboratory look of contemporary cookware. It is the quill vs. the computer — and both are getting their fair share of backers this season.

ABRAHAM & STRAUS, *Willow Grove, PA*

BLOOMINGDALE'S, *King of Prussia, PA*

DAVISON'S, *Atlanta, GA*

LINENS & BATH SHOPS

WOODWARD & LOTHROP, *Baltimore, MD*

Linens are in Show Business — and the Star
names are taking top billing in this area. Special
shops and boutiques are drawing S.R.O. crowds
of fashion-conscious shoppers.

STRAWBRIDGE & CLOTHIER, *Ardmore, PA*

Displays! Dramatic Presentations! Color and Product Coordination! Warm lights and Warmer Settings! It's all Glamour — glow — and glorious merchandising.

ABRAHAM & STRAUS, *Willow Grove, PA*

144

BLOOMINGDALE'S, *King of Prussia, PA*

MACY'S, *Stamford, CT*

ABRAHAM & STRAUS, *King of Prussia, PA*

HECHTS, *Towson, MD*

MACY'S, *Stamford, CT*

146

Fashion dictates — and everybody follows suit. Linens were never lovlier — or more luxurious.

BLOOMINGDALE'S, *King of Prussia, PA*

DESCAMPS, *Washington, D.C.*

MACY'S, *Stamford, CT*

BLOOMINGDALE'S, *King of Prussia, PA*

BULLOCK'S, *1000 Oaks, CA*

The stage is set and the merchandise struts its stuff.
The settings can be semi-realistic or semi-abstract, —
but what counts is the easy to see — easy to combine
and easy to buy merchandise.

ELECTRONICS, TOYS BOOKS, ET AL.

F.A.O. SCHWARZ, *New York, NY*

DAVISON'S, *Atlanta, GA*

STRAWBRIDGE & CLOTHIER, *Burlington, NJ*

Hard goods is getting a soft treatment —
and the treatment is Display and Drama.
"Luggage" is a trip to exciting places, —
"Audio Equipment" & "Computers" are
warmed up for audience acceptance
with low lights and thick carpets, — and
stuffed animals inhabit a wonderful
world all their own.

MACY'S, *Stamford, CT*

Graphics make a glamour statement while the over-sized crayons play-up the small folks area. The myriad T.V. screens are right out of a Sci-Fi epic while the red Book Shop is like no library ever seen before.

BLOOMINGDALE'S, *King of Prussia, PA*

books toys toys books

BAMBERGER'S, *King of Prussia, PA*

STRAWBRIDGE & CLOTHIER, *Burlington, NJ*

MIRADA, *Mexico City, Mexico*

Repetition creates a rhythm that sets the tempo for the shoppers stroll through these areas. Easy to look at, — delightful to hold — and shop.

MACY'S, *New York, NY*

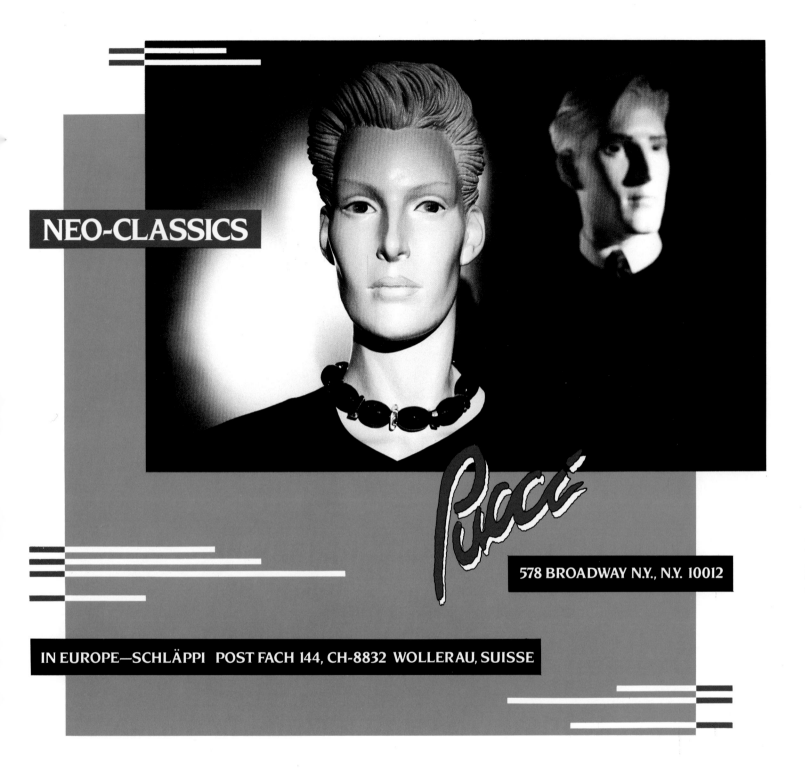

NEO-CLASSICS

Pucci

578 BROADWAY N.Y., N.Y. 10012

IN EUROPE—SCHLÄPPI POST FACH 144, CH-8832 WOLLERAU, SUISSE

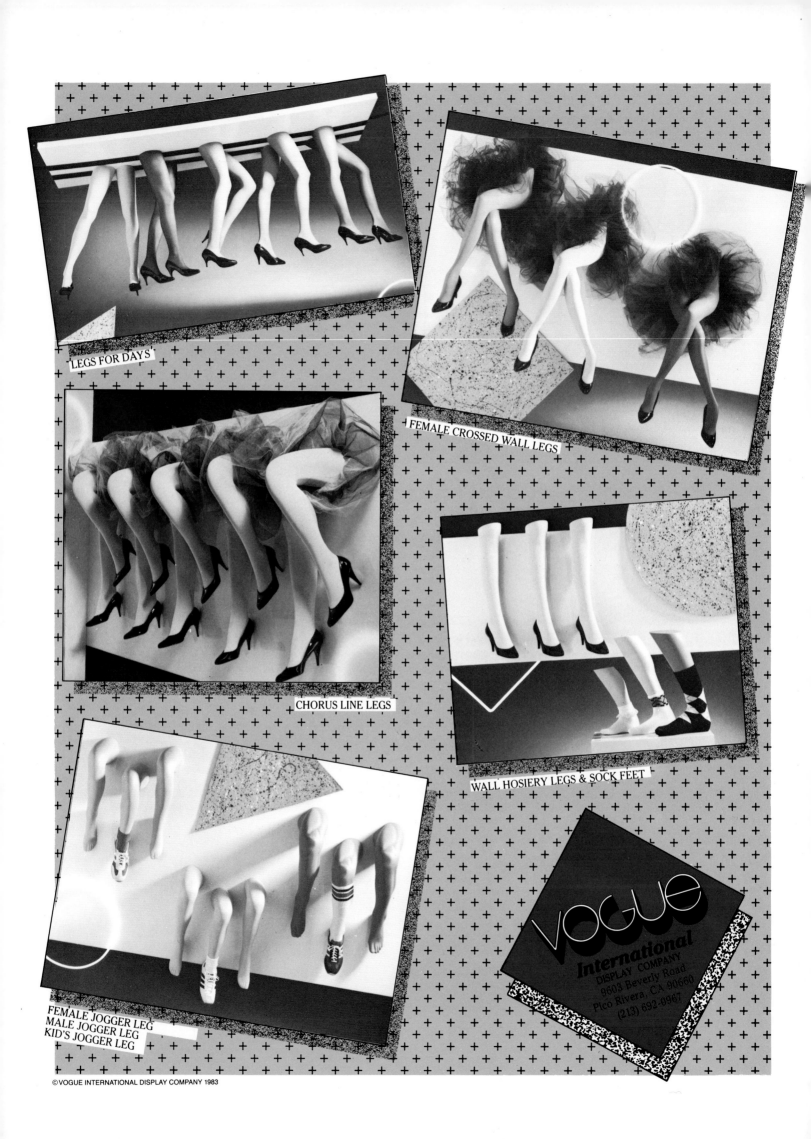

'LEGS FOR DAYS'

FEMALE CROSSED WALL LEGS

CHORUS LINE LEGS

WALL HOSIERY LEGS & SOCK FEET

FEMALE JOGGER LEG
MALE JOGGER LEG
KID'S JOGGER LEG

Vogue
International
DISPLAY COMPANY
9603 Beverly Road
Pico Rivera, CA 90660
(213) 692-0967

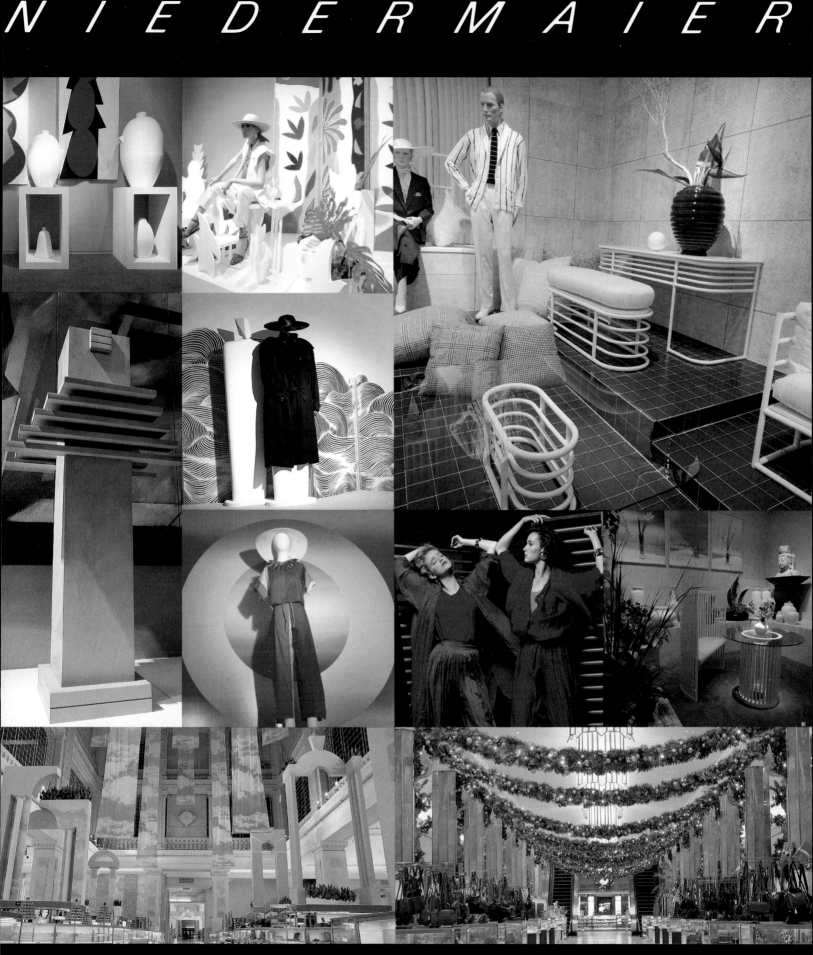

NIEDERMAIER

DECTER

PRESENTS

Fabulous Faces

1118 East Eighth Street, Los Angeles, California 90021 • 11 West Nineteenth Street, New York, New York 10011

Frankie

BY

GEMINI MANNEQUINS

GEMINI MANNEQUINS INC.
23/25 Kensington Park Road, London W11 2EU Tel. 01-229-3843

FRANK GLOVER PRODUCTIONS
Suite 8F 12 East 22nd St. New York City 10010
Tel. 212-473-6455 Please call for appointment

London • New York • Paris • Stuttgart • Kyoto

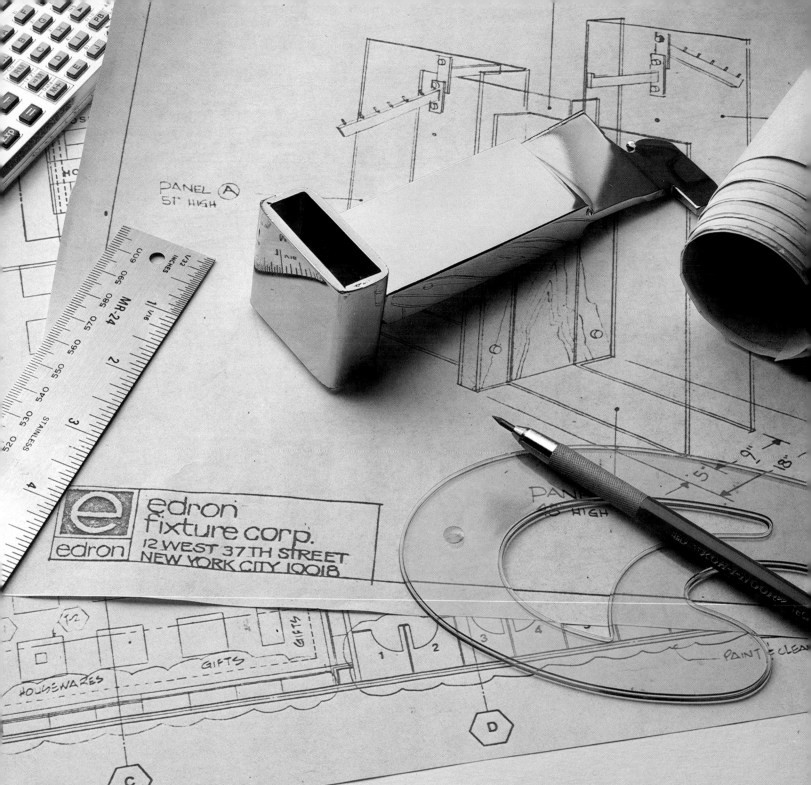

The secret of edron superiority.

Edron. The most trusted name in visual merchandising equipment. Trusted because we've provided "quality control" throughout the years. From custom designing through manufacturing. Making sure every order gets the attention and service it deserves. Every step of the way. Doing it all in our own facilities so we can keep our promises about on-time delivery and most competitive prices. Because it's no secret that we're proud of our reputation of being the best source for visual merchandising equipment and garment racks, anywhere!

Edron Fixture Corp., 11 West 19th St.,
New York City 10011   (212) 741-9100

See us at our new Showroom Location, 5th Floor.

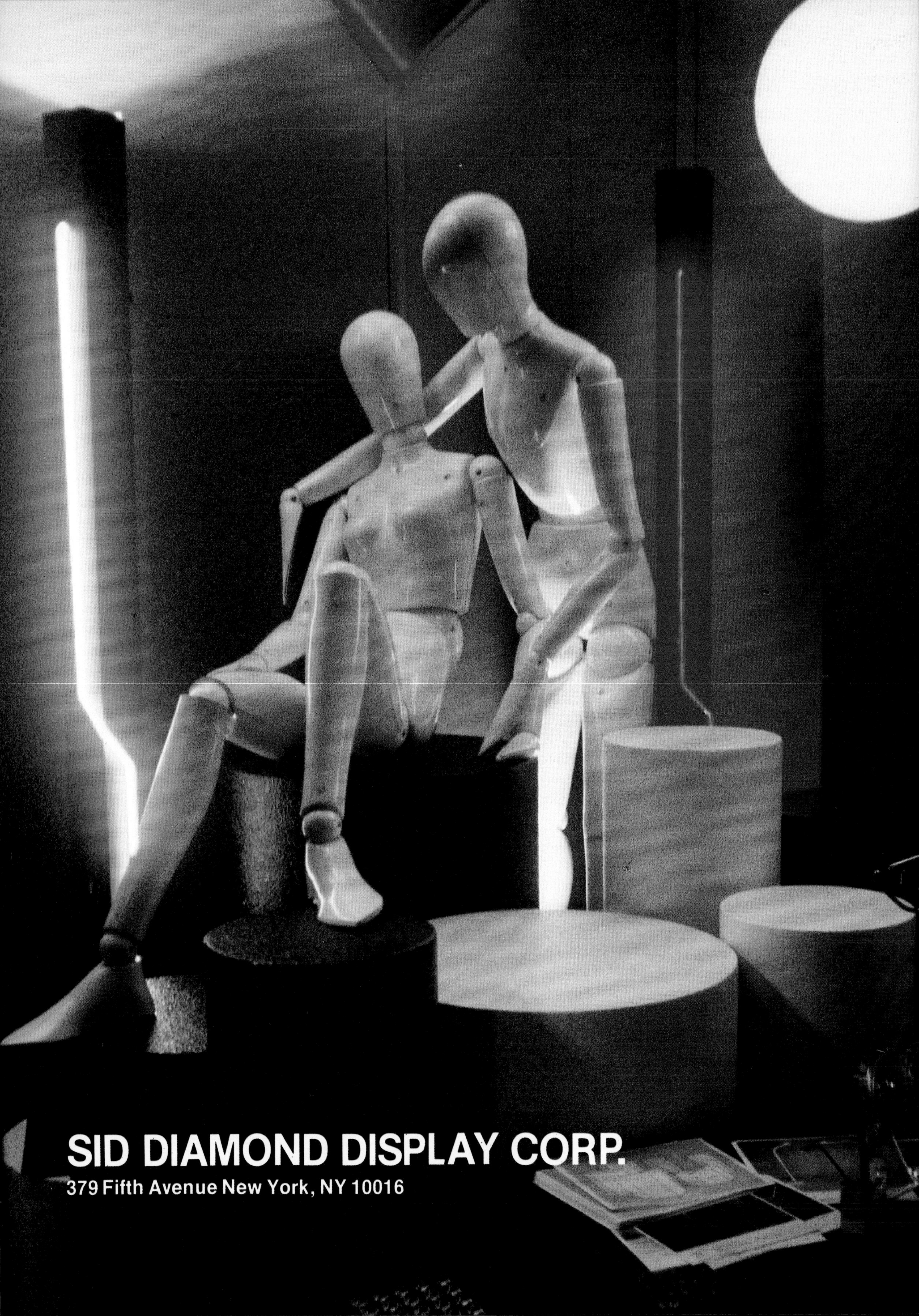
SID DIAMOND DISPLAY CORP.
379 Fifth Avenue New York, NY 10016

If your sphere of interest is visual merchandising, and you are looking for the creative edge . . . keep your eye on the ball. D

Discoveries is one of the largest manufacturers of visual merchandising aids in the United States and has been designing and producing decorative and architectural elements for three generations.

We work in virtually all materials from wood to silk, foam to fiberglass and as you see here with air brush. We mass-produce, import and custom design or produce to your specifications.

Discoveries supplies department and specialty stores, as well as large retail chains, restaurants, hotels, architects and interior designers.

What can we do for you?

Through the years we have earned a reputation for imaginative design and quality production in the visual merchandising field. Many of our clients work with us to create their own designs or modify items we carry in our lines.

See us in our showroom at 120 East 23 Street, Suite 305 when you are in New York. Call us at 212-254-8576 in advance so we can be sure that one of our designers will be there. We are only a phone call away and we are ready and eager to work with you on your ideas.

235 WEST FIRST STREET, BAYONNE, NJ 07002 • SHOWROOM: VMC SUITE #305 — 120 EAST 23RD STREET, NEW YORK, NY 10010 • 212-254-8576

co·gno·scen·ti ltd.

Get More Time To Plan
Your Merchandising Success

Spend less time tracking down suppliers. One, time-saving phone call puts an entire package of retail design products at your fingertips. Beautiful, functional Marlite® Brand products, coordinated from one expert source of supply. One set of shipping instructions. One invoice. Less time spent spinning your wheels to get stores opened on time.

Marlite Brand products . . . they'll help you find more time to plan your merchandising success.

Displawall™: The best value in slotted wall systems. Backed by our "Fast Track Service" Program.

Displamates™: Attractive, fast-changing, free-standing displays.

Presentation Accessories: Metal and acrylic fixtures for use with Displawall and Displamates.

Plank: Pre-finished, 16″ wide wall coverings in beautifully textured woodgrain designs that won't look used the first time they're touched. Also, high gloss solids to add excitement and perfectly match the most modern colors for case goods.

Linear Wood Ceilings: Featuring a unique installation system that makes real wood ceilings affordable.

And more. Make one convenient phone call to your nearest Commercial Division Regional Operations Center, today.

COMMERCIAL DIVISION

MASONITE CORPORATION

Commercial Division Regional Operations Centers are located in:
Dover, Ohio 216/343-6621 • Edison, New Jersey 201/225-1650 • Atlanta, Georgia 404/355-1980 • Fort Worth, Texas 817/625-6443 • LaMirada, California 714/523-2500, 213/944-0157

NATIONAL ASSOCIATION OF DISPLAY INDUSTRIES

Two exciting visual merchandising markets each year in June and December featuring over 225 exhibits. For complete show information, write:

NATIONAL ASSOCIATION OF DISPLAY INDUSTRIES
120 E.23rd St.,N.Y.NY 10010
212-982-6571

You are invited to join some of the best creative minds in store planning...

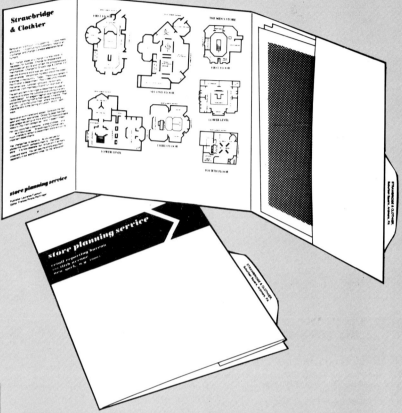

RETAIL REPORTING BUREAU 101 Fifth Avenue New York, New York 10003

MACY'S, Herald Square, New York   Neat and tailored, the working women's favorites are gathered together in this important shop on Macy's Third Floor. The classic nature of the merchandise is brought a colorful and exciting element with the ethnic appeal. Richly neutral color on all surfaces and beamed ceiling work together creating an appealing impression and a perfect place for a variety of merchandise.   81-272S

SUITS/COORDINATES

RETAIL REPORTING BUREAU 101 Fifth Avenue New York, New York 10003

ANN TAYLOR
The Court at King of Prussia, PA
Architect: Charles E. Brody
& Associates., Phil. PA
Contractor: Ford Building, Inc., 82-179
Ivar Kasaks, N.Y.,N.Y.
Visual Pres. Dir.:Sonny Jaen

Sleek, inviting lines draw us into Ann Taylor. Architecture flows easily from space to space. Rich wood floor, accent ceiling, walls and fixtures follow suit, creating an arrangement to enhance customer traffic flow.   82-179
COPYRIGHT©

"Make your selling space into a sparkling selling environment."

There's never been a publication like Store Planning Service. It's a unique publication concerned solely with keeping professionals like you up to date with new store design. By subscribing to Store Planning Service you receive 30 8x10 full color photos per month showing new merchandising concepts — the most recent stores, new installations and rehabs. You'll see new trends and directions as they're developing...the latest techniques — new materials, fixtures, lighting, interior design, visual merchandising and display. Subscribe to Store Planning Service at the rate of $45.00 per month plus postage.

Our Guarantee: If you feel Store Planning Service does not live up to your expectations you can cancel at any time for any reason. For overseas subscription write for the agent in your area.

Subscribe today, call toll free 800-251-4545 or write:

Retail Reporting Bureau 101 Fifth Ave New York, N.Y. 10003 212•255-9595

DESIGNER CREDITS

Listed on these pages, in alphabetical order, are many stores which are shown in the preceding pages. Where permitted, we have listed the individual and/or design firms who were involved in the design and planning.

ABRAHAM & STRAUS, King of Prussia, PA
Interior: Robert Young Associates, New York, Dallas, TX
ABRAHAM & STRAUS, Willow Grove, PA
Design: Robert Young Assoc., New York, Dallas, TX
ANN TAYLOR, Bal Harbour, FL
Architect: Charles E. Broudy & Assoc., Philadelphia, PA
Principal in Charge: Charles Broudy, Project Architect:
Charles King, V.P. Store Planning: Ivar Kasaks, Vis. Mdsg.
Director: Sonny Jaen
ANN TAYLOR, Boston, MA & Crystal Palace, NY
Architect: Charles E. Broudy & Assoc., Philadelphia, PA, Principal in Charge: Charles Broudy, Project Architect: Charles
King, V.P. Store Planning: Ivar Kasaks, Vis. Mdsg. Director:
Sonny Jaen
ANN TAYLOR, Willow Grove, PA
Architect: Charles E. Broudy & Assoc., Philadelphia, PA,
Vis. Pres. Director: Sonny Jaen
ATHLEISURE, King of Prussia, PA
Design: Stephen Sanders & Assoc., Manhasset, NY
B. ALTMAN & CO., Willow Grove, PA
Interior: C.J. Breyer & Assoc., NY, B. Altman & Co. Store
Planning: George Keller, William Rufo, B. Altman & Co.
Display: Andrew Druschilowsky
BAMBERGER'S, Livingston, NJ
Interior Design: CNI Intl. Inc., NY, Bamberger's Store Planning
& Design Departments, F. Richard Clemente, V.P. Store Planning & Project Management: Virginia Moraweck, V.P. Store
Design: Thomas Zupich, Store Planning Project Coordinator,
Judy Schuler, Design Coordinator
BAMBERGER'S, King of Prussia, PA
Interior: The Schwartzman & Tucci Consultants Inc., NY
BANBURY CROSS, New York, NY
Designer: Frank Garofolo, NY
BARNEY'S, New York, NY
Design: Peter Morino, NY
BATA INTERNATIONAL, Vina del Mar, Chile
Project Prep: Bata Limited, Design Studio, Toronto, Designer:
Maria Lisowicz
BLOOMINGDALE'S, King of Prussia, PA
Architect: Helmuth, Obata & Kassabaum, NY, Design: Norwood Oliver Design Assoc., NY and Barbara D'Arcy, Bloomingdale's V.P. & Dir. of Mdsg. Pres.
BODY DESIGNS, Stamford, CT
Architectural Design: The Design Circle, New York, NY
BONWIT TELLER, Manhasset, NY
Interior: Allied Store Planning, NY, V.P. Dir. Vis. Mdsg. & Store
Planning: Frank C. Calise
BRANDEIS, Omaha, NE
Interior Design: Tucci, Segrete & Rosen, New York, NY, Jim
Dennings, Brandeis Store Planning
THE BROADWAY, Los Angeles, CA
Interior/Architectural Design: MTH Design Group, a division of
Swimmer Cole Martinez Curtis, Marina del Rey, CA, Coordinating Architect: Associated Architects & Planners,
Los Angeles, CA
BULLOCK'S, Manhattan Beach, CA
Design: Bullock's Store Planning, A Division of Federated
Department Stores
BULLOCK'S, Thousand Oaks, CA
Interior Design: CNI Intl., Inc., NY, Bullock's Store Planning
Staff and their Consultants

BYCK'S, Louisville, KY
Interior Design: CNI International Inc. NY, Lawrence J. Israel,
A.I.A. President, Andre C. Ruellan I.S.P., V.P. in charge, Edward Calabrese, Designer, Susan Starnes, Decorator
CANDIE'S BAR, White Plains, NY
Design: D.I. Retail Planning & Design, NY
CARNAVAL, New York, NY
Architect & Design: Michael Rosenberg
CLAIRE PEARONE, Troy, MI
Interior Design: Jon Greenberg & Associates, Berkley, MI
CLOTHES TO BOOT, New York, NY
Design: Al Martinez, NY
DAIMURA, Osaka, Japan
Design & Visual Concepts: Chaix & Johnson Architects,
Los Angeles, CA
DANCE CENTRE, New York, NY
Design: Linda Hall Chase
DAVID CRAIG, Langhorne, PA
Project Designer: Studio +, New York, NY, Project Principals:
Ron Pompeii, Paul Golden
DAVIDSON'S, Atlanta, GA
Interior Design: CNI International, Inc., NY
DAYTON'S, St. Paul, MN
R.J. Pavlik Design Team, Ft. Lauderdale, Andrew J.
Markopoulos, Vice President Visual Merchandising & Design,
James Seyko, Divisional Vice President Store Planning & Construction
D.D.L. FOOD SHOW, New York, NY
Architect: Adam Tihani, NY
DEAN & DE LUCA, New York, NY
Architect: Jack Ceglic, NY
THE DENVER, Denver, CO
Interior Design: The Pavlik Design Team, Ft. Lauderdale, FL
DESIGNER ONE LINGERIE, Larchmont, NY
Interior Design: D.M. Hecht Assoc., NY
DIANNE B., New York, NY
Architect: Ed Mills, Voorslanger & Mills, New York, NY
ERELLA, West Bloomfield, MI
Interior Design: Jon Greenberg & Associates, Berkley, MI
FAO SCHWARZ, New York, NY
Design: Naomi Leff & Associates, Inc., NY
FIELD BROTHERS, Willowbrook, NJ
Design: Rubano Mirviss Assoc., New York, NY
FIELD BROTHERS, Huntington, NY
Design: Rubano Mirviss Assoc., New York, NY
FILENE'S, Newington, NH
Interior Design: Norwood Oliver Design Assoc., New York, NY
FILENE'S, Boston, MA
Interior Design: Norwood Oliver Design Assoc., New York, NY
& Visual Merchandising Divisions.
FOLEY'S, Memorial City, Houston, TX
Design: Foley's Store Planning & Design
FREDERIC GOODMAN, Upper Montclair, NJ
Interior Design: D.I. Retail Planning & Design, New York, NY
FURLA, New York, NY
Architect: Piero Polato, Milan
THE GAP STORES INC., Paramus, NJ
Architecture/Interior Design: Walker Group, New York, NY
GIVENCHY, New York, NY
Design: Hubert de Givenchy in conjunction with John Rizzuto,
President, Givenchy Inc. and Curt Gareth, Creative Director,
Givenchy Inc.
HECHT'S, Towson, MD
Interior: R.Y.A., Dallas in cooperation with Hecht's Store Planning & Visual Merchandising Divisions

HIGH GEAR, New York, NY
Architect & Designer: John Schaffner
HIGH VOLTAGE, Dallas, TX
Design: William Horton, Dallas, TX
HOLT RENFREW, Edmonton, Canada
Interior Design: Norwood Oliver Design Assoc., New York, NY
HUTZLER'S, Baltimore, MD
Architect:RTKL & Assoc. Ind., Baltimore, MD, Planning &
Design: Pfeiffer & Miro Assoc., NY
JEWEL MART, Akron, OH
Design: Howard Garrett & Assoc., Birmingham, AL
JOHN HOGAN, Newport Beach, CA
Architect: Mayer/Taylor Assoc., and Pacific-Five, a Division of
Mayer/Taylor, Santa Monica, CA
JOSEPH MAGNIN, Torrance, CA
Design: Planning and Design Concepts, San Francisco, CA
KNIT WIT, Willow Grove, PA
Project Designer; Studio +, New York, NY, Project Principals:
Ron Pompeii, Karen Bausman, Leslie Gill, Project Architect:
Schlosser-Rivera-Krumholz, Philadelphia, PA
LE SPORTSAC, New York, NY
Design: Carr & Associates, Los Angeles, CA
LOEWE, Trump Tower, NY
Design: Weisberg Castro Assoc., in coordination with Jacques
Blond and the Loewe Design Group, NY
LONDON JEWELERS, Greenvale, NY
Design: Stephen Sanders & Assoc., Manhasset, NY
LONNY'S, Woodbury, NY
Design: Jab Store Interiors, Arthur Bloom; Southgate
Interiors, Tom Edwards; Lonny's, Lon Goldstein; Stephen
Sander & Assoc., Manhasset, NY
LORD & TAYLOR, North Miami, FL
Interior Design: The Pavlik Design Team, Ft. Lauderdale, FL
LULU'S, New York, NY
Architect: Michael Russo
MACY'S, Stamford, CT
Interior Design: Macy's NY Visual Merchandising & Store Planning, CNI International Inc., NY
MAMMINA, Tokyo, Japan
Planning/Interior Design: Chaix & Johnson Architects,
Los Angeles, CA
MANSOURI, Greenvale, NY
Design: Stephen Sanders & Assoc., Manhasset, NY
MARSHALL FIELD & CO., Chicago, IL
Design: Marshall Field & Co., Store Planning & Design
Division
MARSHALL FIELD & CO., Dallas, TX
Design: Walker/Group, NY
MARVIN RICHARDS, Woodbury, NY
Design: Stephen Sanders & Assoc., Manhasset, NY
MATSUYA, Tokyo, Japan
Design & Visual Concepts: Chaix & Johnson Architects,
Los Angeles, CA
THE MAY CO., Palm Desert, CA
Design: May Design & Construction St. Louis, MO, Visual
Presentation: Branch Store, Presentation Dir.: Linden Phelps
Holmes, V.P. Vis. Mdsg. Pres.: May Co., California,
Peter Shyne
MIRADA, Mexico City, Mexico
Design, Execution: Direction, S.A. de C.V., Samuel Podolsky
and Bronia Nosnik of Mexico City
MOI LE CHIC, Woodbury, NY
Design: Stephen Sanders & Assoc., Manhasset, NY
THE MUSEUM STORE, Field Museum, Chicago, IL
Design: Trauth Associates, Chicago, IL

NIKE ONLY STORE, Beaverton, OR
Corporate Architect: Tinker Hatfield, Display: Palaniuk
Display, Portland, OR
NORDSTROM, San Diego, CA
Architects/Designers: The Callison Partnership, Seattle,
WA/Portland, OR
NORDSTROM, Bellevue, WA
Architects/Designers: The Callison Partnership, Seattle,
WA/Portland, OR
OVERTURES, Brooklyn Heights, NY
Interior Design: D.I. Retail Planning & Design, New York, NY
PALACIO DE HIERRO, Mexico City, Mexico
Interior Design: CNI International, INC., New York, NY
PEANUTS, West Bloomfield, MI
Interior Design: Jon Greenberg & Associates, Berkley, MI
PIED PIPER, Manhasset, NY
Design: Stephen Sanders & Assoc., Manhasset, NY
ROBSON LTD, Cherry Hill, NJ
Design: Stephen Sanders & Assoc., Manhasset, NY
ROSSETTI, New York, NY
Design: Piero Pinto, Venice
SAFEWAY, Broken Arrow, OK
Planning & Design: The Doody Company, Columbus, OH
SAKS FIFTH AVENUE, Dallas, TX
Designed by HTI and James E. Terrell, NY, Decor by Batus
Retail, Project Administrator: Ray Nuytkens, Project
Coordinator: Michael L. Kirn.
SEALFONS, Ridgewood, NJ
Design: Rubano Mirviss Assoc., New York, NY
SIBLEY'S, Rochester, NY
Interior Design: CNI Intl., NY, Lawrence J. Israel, A.I.A. President Andre C. Ruellan, I.S.P., V.P. in charge, Thomas A.
Tarnowski, Designer
STRAWBRIDGE & CLOTHIER, Burlington, NJ
Design: RTKL Associates, Baltimore, MD and the Pavlik
Design Team, Ft. Lauderdale, FL
STRAWBRIDGE & CLOTHIER, Ardmore, PA
Interior Design: Norwood Oliver Design Assoc., New York, NY
STREETS & CO., New York, NY
Architect: Stephen Wood, New York
TO BOOT, New York, NY
Design: Al Martinez, New York
TOP SHOP, Cambridge, England
Design: Fitch & Company, London
TRUMP TOWER, New York, NY
Architect: Swanke, Hayden Connell and Partners, NY, Design
Architect: Der Scutt
ULTRA FEMME, Cancuun, Mexico
Design: Elizabeth Yates, Coral Gables, FL
UPPER MAD, New York, NY
Design: Larry Zim & Mel Lerner, Zim-Lerner Inc., New York
VITTORIO RICCI, New York, NY
Design: Peter Morino, NY
WOLFMAN GOLD & GOODS CO., New York, NY
Architect: Charles Swerz, NY, Designer: Peri Wolfman
WOODWARD & LOTHROP, Baltimore, MD
Interior: The Pavlik Design Team, Ft. Lauderdale, FL
YOUNKERS, Des Moines, IA
Design: Schafer Assoc., Oak Brook, IL, Corporate Architect,
Younkers: Kurt Christansen, Dir. of Vis. Mdsg.: James Spitznagel
YVES SAINT LAURENT, Manhasset, NY
Design: Stephen Sanders & Assoc., Manhasset, NY
ZOOM, New York, NY
Design: Larry Laslo, New York
ZOO SHOP, Lincoln Park Zoo, Chicago, IL
Design: Trauth Associates, Chicago, IL